STREET PHOTOGRAPHY

POCKET GUIDE

TABLE OF CONTENTS

I0737543

PRE-SHOOT CHECKLIST

Check these settings before you head out with your camera!

SETTING	MY PREFERRED SETTING
☑ Exposure Mode	....
☑ Exposure Compensation	....
☑ ISO	....
☑ White Balance	....
☑ Focus Mode and Point	....
☑ Drive Mode	....
☑ Metering Mode	....
☑ Image Bracketing	....
☑ Image Quality and Size	....
☑ Image Stabilization	....
☑ Electronic/Mechanical Shutter	....
☑ Silent Shooting Mode	....
☑ Sleep Function	....
☑ Flash Mode	....
☑ Battery Fully Charged and In Camera	....
☑ Memory Card(s) Formatted and In Camera	....
☑ Extra Batteries and/or Rolls of Film	....

01 STREET PHOTOGRAPHY FUNDAMENTALS

WHAT IS STREET PHOTOGRAPHY?

Now there's a controversial question to start things off! For the purposes of this Pocket Guide, we'll take a fairly broad definition: a good starting point is "candid public photography."

This amounts to photographing unstaged, unmediated encounters in public spaces. Does a street photo always need to include people? Usually, yes, but there's no hard and fast rule; sometimes an implication or suggestion of humanity will suffice.

One of the difficulties we encounter as street photographers is how to make our world look interesting—and herein lies one of the problems with the genre. We have all seen boring pictures of a man crossing the road, someone sitting in a café window, a busker, or a homeless person. Are these scenes remotely interesting? Usually not, and they need something to elevate them to something worthy of our attention—and that something is usually a "moment." But more on that later.

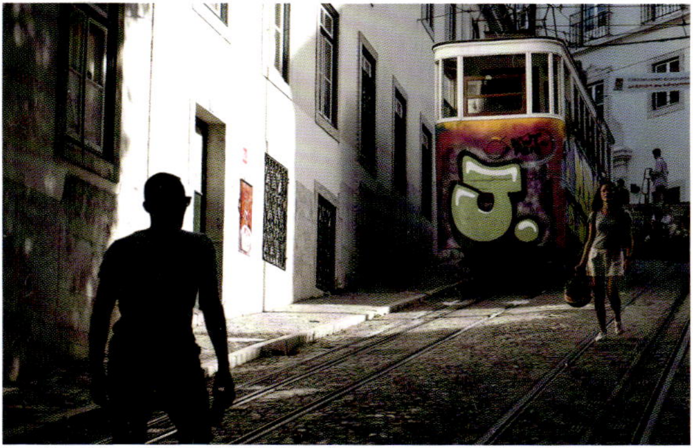

As street photographers we must be a combination of observer, flâneur, storyteller, and aestheticist. We live in the moment, always searching for ways to connect with the world through the medium of photography.

There are some personality traits commonly found in successful street photographers: we tend to be curious, patient, observant, brave, tenacious, creative, mischievous, humorous, open-minded, and driven. If you score 10 out of 10 on these success factors, you've certainly got what it takes!

We can practice our art almost anywhere, from the biggest city to the smallest town—and even at places like the beach. We can shoot at any time of the day or night, in any weather and whatever the season. And we don't need masses of gear to do it: just one camera, one lens, and a couple of batteries (or rolls of film).

If you're new to street photography, you're embarking on an exciting journey with serendipitous surprises around every corner; stay the course and you'll be amply rewarded. If you're already an experienced street photographer, you'll appreciate that there's something new to learn with every day spent on the streets.

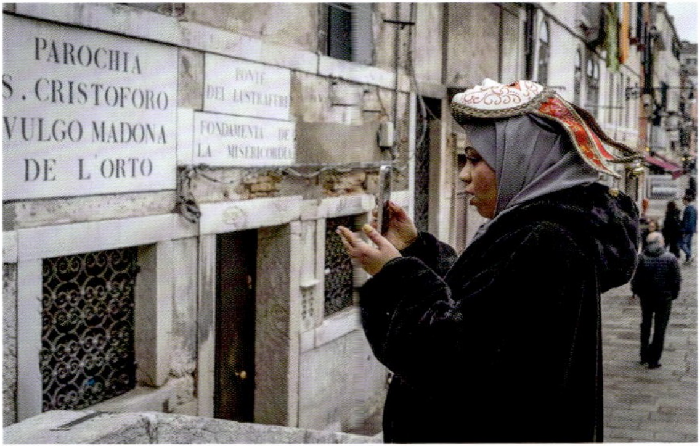

THREE APPROACHES TO STREET PHOTOGRAPHY

We all see the streets differently and you will, through trial, error, and experimentation, find an approach that works for you. Over the years, street photographers have approached their work in a great many ways but, to keep things simple, let's distill this down into three approaches: the "moment," the "aesthetic," and the "narrative."

These approaches are not mutually exclusive, and it's quite feasible to adopt all three—but you may find yourself drawn to one of them, and this is always a good starting point.

The "Moment" Approach

Think Henri Cartier-Bresson, Garry Winogrand, and Elliott Erwitt: they were the "classical" street photographers, for whom some kind of "moment" made the image work. There's often humor inherent in this style—or at least a sense of irony, mischief, or playfulness.

To make this approach work you must be alert to your surroundings, quick to react, and open-minded to the possibilities in a scene. This approach is great fun and highly rewarding, but it's a long game—don't expect lots of quick or easy wins.

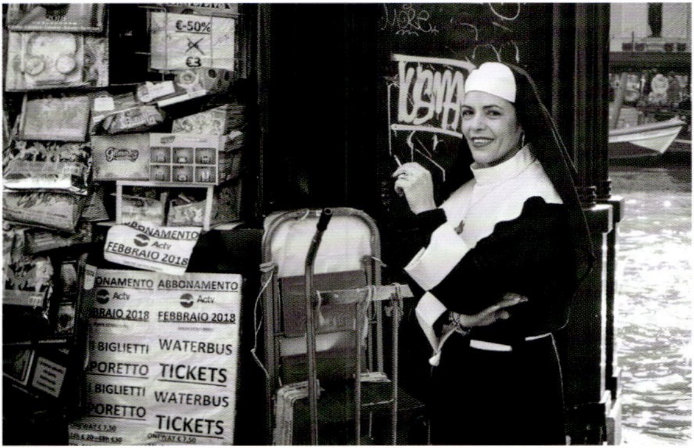

"Oop! The Moment! Once you miss it, it is gone forever."

Henri Cartier-Bresson

What to look out for:

- People doing odd things—or acting out of context
- The "unusual in the usual" or "beauty in the mundane"
- Contrasts (tall/short, red/green, happy/sad, etc.)
- Juxtapositions
- Repetitions (of form, color, pattern, etc.)
- Word play: using words/signs to make connections

- Connections: where two or more elements in the frame work with each other, often to humorous effect

So if you're naturally drawn to humor, whimsy, or perhaps even mischief, this could be the approach for you. For inspiration, also check out the work of Joel Meyerowitz, William Klein, Daido Moriyama, and Matt Stuart.

The Aesthetic Approach

This approach all started with Saul Leiter and his stylish abstract images of the New York streets. It's all about the visual appeal of an image; there may be no "moment" and no story—but there will be strong visual elements such as color, form, or striking graphical qualities.

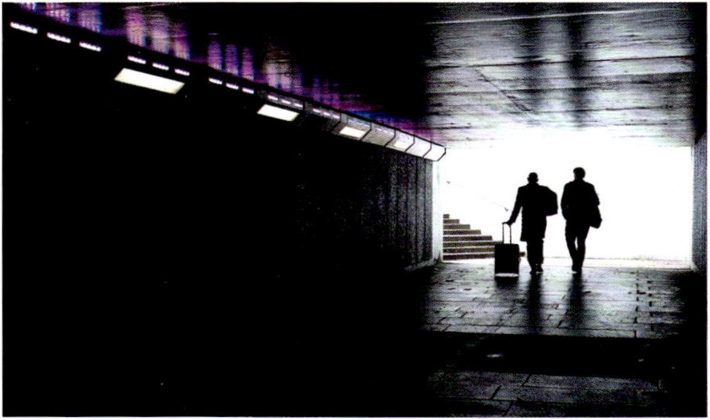

"A window covered with raindrops interests me more than a photograph of a famous person."

Saul Leiter

What to look out for:

- Strong colors (red or yellow is usually a good starting point)
- Dramatic or interesting light
- Silhouettes and shadows
- Large areas of negative space
- Layers you can shoot through, such as misted-up windows
- Severe weather (Leiter worked a lot in rain and snow)
- The potential to make an abstract

This is a great approach if you don't feel confident shooting people, or perhaps if there's an inner artist in you. You'll find plenty of inspiration in the work of Leiter, Ernst Haas, and Fan Ho.

The Narrative Approach

This approach is all about storytelling. It's that interesting space where street photography meets documentary photography. From Robert Frank in the 1950s to Martin Parr today, with his social documentary work, we can see how life on the streets can be crystallized into stories. Story-based street photography is a consuming and absorbing passion, and it's best done through the medium of projects (see Part 5: Shoot Projects).

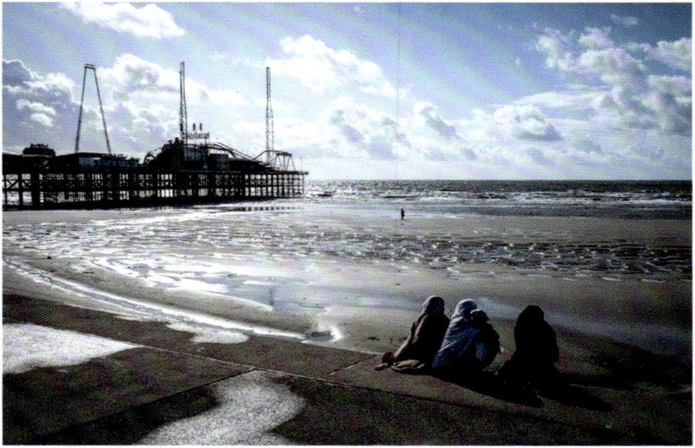

"When people look at my pictures I want them to feel the way they do when they want to read a line of a poem twice."

Robert Frank

What to look out for: This is more about "pre-meditated" street photography, where you hit the streets with an idea for your story; you should have a pretty good idea of what you're looking for.

If you're the sort of photographer who needs to tell a story, get a message across, or make a point, this may be the approach for you. Check out the work of Robert Frank, Walker Evans, and Tony Ray-Jones for inspiration.

WHICH CAMERA?

One of the great things about street photography is that you can do it with just about any camera, and you don't need to buy lots of expensive gear. The ideal camera is small, light, and discreet—a mirrorless rangefinder style camera is the top choice for many street photographers. But whatever you have—DSLR, compact, mirrorless, or even a film camera—will do the job.

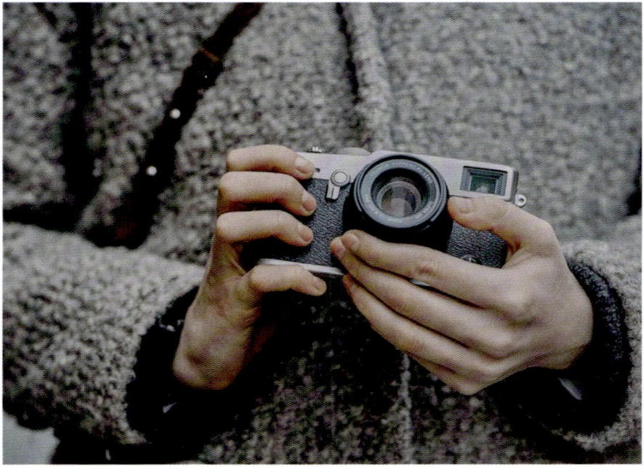

LENS CHOICE

Because context is often an important factor in a street shot, a wide lens is the preferred choice. Most street photographers shoot at 28mm or 35mm; the 50mm lens has always been popular and, if you're uncomfortable about getting close to people, this may be a good place to start. However, the 35mm is probably the "sweet spot" and, if you were to use only one lens, it should probably be this one.

As we usually shoot at f/8 or smaller, choose lightweight and weather-sealing over a wide maximum aperture (such as f/2).

It's best to take only one lens out with you. Get used to what that lens sees and to how it describes the world—this will make you a more intuitive and spontaneous street photographer. Constantly changing lenses is distracting and takes your attention away from what's happening in front of you.

WHAT'S IN YOUR BAG?

Always travel light for a day on the streets—in fact, many street photographers don't carry a bag at all and just leave home with a few batteries and a spare memory card in their pockets. However, it's good to have the basics covered:

- Spare batteries
- Memory cards
- Notebook and pen
- Lens cloth/wipes
- Business cards
- Map and/or location notes

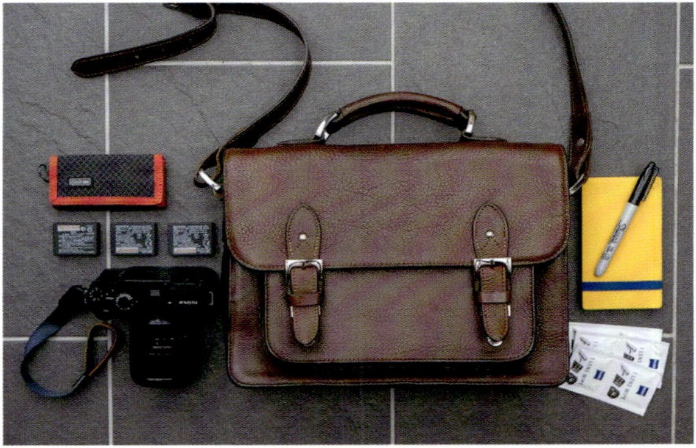

CHOOSING A LOCATION

Locations will depend on what sort of shots you're aiming to achieve. Some depend on interesting light; others require lots of people; some situations are background-specific. For most purposes it's generally a good idea to head to places that are well populated, well lit, and offer plenty of opportunities to observe a wide variety of street scenes; town squares or street corners are great places for this.

PLANNING

Don't hit the streets without a plan! You'll have a much more fulfilling day if you know what sort of shots you're looking for, have researched the location, and know roughly where you're heading. While leaving it all to chance is sometimes spontaneous and fun, you'll be more productive if you have some themes or projects in mind (see Part 5 for more on this).

WEATHER & LIGHT

Bright sunshine is what most street photographers hope for. A sunny day gives us more to play with: high contrast, shadows, silhouettes, and wonderfully saturated colors. But you shouldn't ever be a "fair weather" street shooter. Don't be put off by adverse weather—some great street images can be shot in rain, snow, fog, or strong winds—and you can use these conditions to your advantage and will be able to add drama or atmosphere to your pictures.

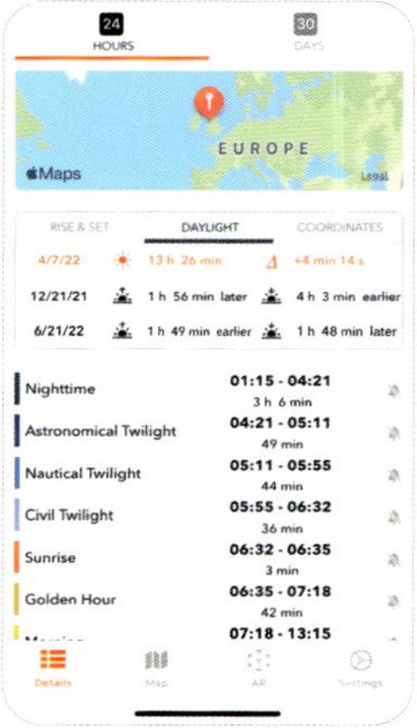

Apps such as PhotoPills or Sun Tracker are great for helping you calculate the sun's position and path as well has helping with the timing of your trip.

02 CAMERA SETUP

EXPOSURE SETTINGS: SET IT AND FORGET IT!

Whatever camera you're using, you need to be able to operate it quickly and without thinking. All your attention should be focused on what's happening around you—not on camera dials, buttons, and menus.

It's good practice to have your camera set up in such a way that you'll get the shot 98% of the time; the shot may not always be perfect but in street photography that's fine—we're much more concerned about getting the shot than we are about perfection.

So your "standard" street settings should go something like this:

- **Exposure mode: Aperture Priority**
- **Aperture: f/8**
- **ISO: Auto** (set the range to 200–6400 with a minimum shutter speed of 1/200 sec.)

With these settings you'll be equipped to handle most situations on the streets. Don't worry if the ISO runs to a high level—it's much better to have a tiny bit of noise than a picture that's ruined because there wasn't enough light.

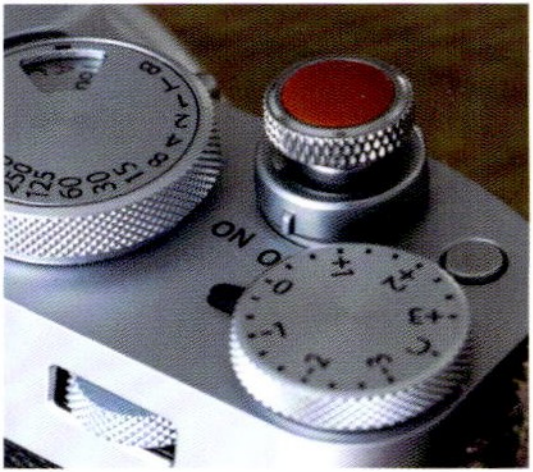

Now for the game-changer! There will be times when you need to make adjustments to the exposure to adapt to different lighting conditions, and you can do this very quickly using the **Exposure Compensation** dial. Use this to make quick tweaks on the fly, either shutting light out of the camera (a minus setting) or letting more light in (a positive setting). Once you get used to this, you'll find it the fastest and most instinctive way to manipulate your exposure.

Of course, you can quickly change those settings for changing situations—such as when a shaft of sunlight suddenly hits the street—or maybe to achieve a shallow depth of field for a street portrait (see Part 4: Street Portraits).

FOCUSING

As with the exposure settings, speed is of the essence. Modern cameras have very good autofocus (AF), which works fine in most situations. Which AF mode you choose doesn't really matter, though the simplest—"single point AF"—is usually best.

However, many street photographers find it much quicker to focus manually using **zone focusing**. This simply means turning off your AF and manually setting the focus in advance. And then, when your subject comes into range, you press the shutter button and you've got a sharp image. To do this, you ideally need a wide-angle prime lens (35mm or wider is ideal). The wider the lens—and the smaller the aperture—the greater the "zone" that's in focus. Here's an example:

- 28mm lens
- Manually set the focus distance at 9 feet (3 meters)
- Set the aperture at f/8

Although the precise figures will vary according to your camera/lens combination, you'll find that your zone (the range of what's in focus) will be around 5–25 feet; as long as your main subject falls within that range it will be sharp.

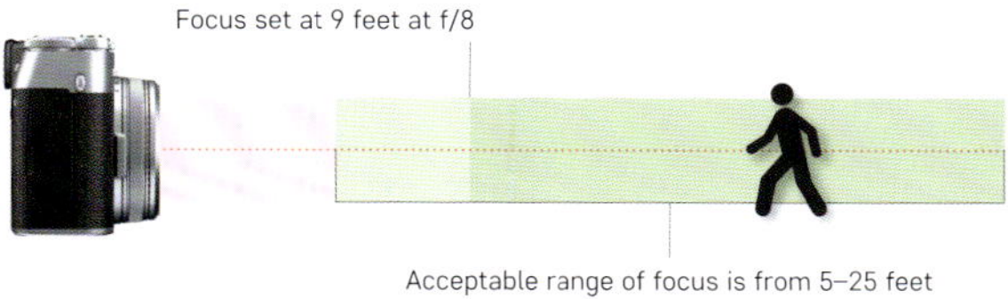

Some street photographers use the combination of zone focusing and back-button focusing, which perhaps offers the best of both worlds. Back-button focusing separates and removes the focus function from the shutter button; the shutter button will now only take the picture—firing the shutter once fully depressed—and focusing is achieved using a button on the back of the camera—usually the AF-On button.

Zone focusing is liberating and, combined with the above exposure settings, it allows you to concentrate fully on your subjects and be free from any technical distractions.

OTHER CAMERA SETTINGS

- **File format:** It's best to shoot in **RAW** so that you'll have more flexibility in post-production if you need it.
- **White balance:** Set it to **Auto** as you'll probably have numerous and different light sources to contend with.
- **Metering: Evaluative or Matrix** usually gets it right. Some people use Spot metering but I think it takes up too much valuable reaction time.
- **Drive mode:** You can shoot in **Single Shot or Continuous** mode, although street photography purists would generally avoid the latter as it feels like "cheating"!
- **Image stabilization:** If you have it, use it!

OTHER CONSIDERATIONS

- So that you can work discreetly and stealthily, **switch off anything that makes a noise**, such as the exposure lock "beep"; also **disable any blinking lights**.
- You'll want your camera to always be "awake" for any unexpected moments, so **disable the "sleep" function** (and carry a few extra batteries to compensate).
- **Use electronic (silent) shutter mode** if you have one (though not if you're shooting in artificial light, as it can cause banding).
- Street photography is all about authenticity, so try to **avoid relying on in-camera special effects or film simulations**. Keep things natural!
- Try to **avoid "chimping"** (reviewing the image on your LCD playback screen). This takes your attention away from what's happening around you and could draw attention to the fact that you've just taken a picture.

03 STREET TECHNIQUES

DEVELOP YOUR STREET MINDSET

There's only one way to be good that this—and that's full immersion: you need to live, think, and act like a street photographer! And it's not as challenging as it sounds.

There are several traits shared by successful street photographers: some of these are inherent within us, and some are acquired with patience and practice. None of these are outside anyone's reach and, over time, they will become part of your street mindset. It's the photographer's version of being "streetwise."

Be Happy!

Always have open, positive, and friendly body language. The "happy" street photographer tends to have far fewer confrontations and a much easier time on the streets.

Stay in the Zone

Make sure you're alert and tuned in to what's happening around you; concentration is vital, so leave your phone in your pocket and turn your music off.

Never Hesitate

As soon as you see the potential for a picture, hit that shutter button! Don't overthink it. React quickly and spontaneously to events. Shoot first and think later.

Anticipate

Watch people intently and study their body language. You always need to be thinking, "What's going to happen next?"

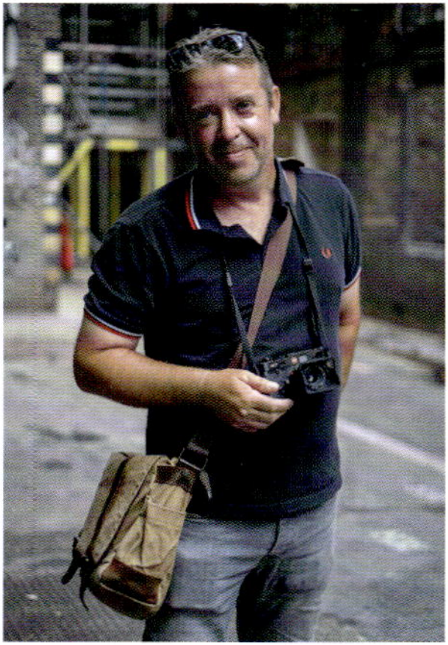

Take Your Time

Walk slowly and don't rush from one location to the next. If you take your time to observe what's happening around you, you'll "see" so much more.

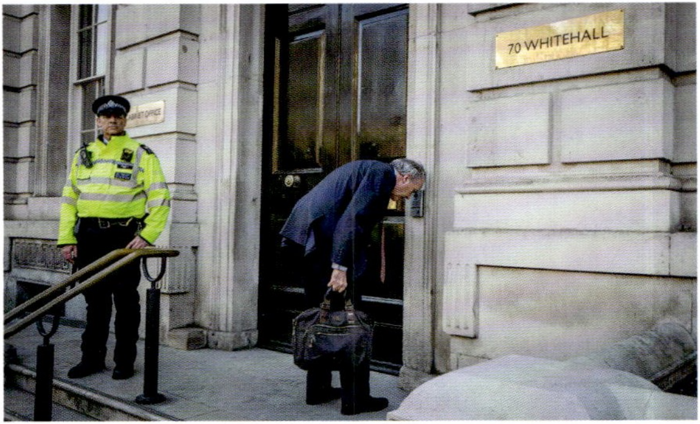

Find the Detail

We need to have great observational skills, and part of that skillset is being able to spot relevant or interesting detail we can use to make an interesting or witty picture.

Make Connections

By connecting things together in a frame you'll be bringing another dimension to your images. A simple (and cliched) example is a picture of a guy smoking next to a "No Smoking" sign.

Be Curious

You need to be nosy! A strong sense of curiosity opens up many more picture-taking opportunities for you.

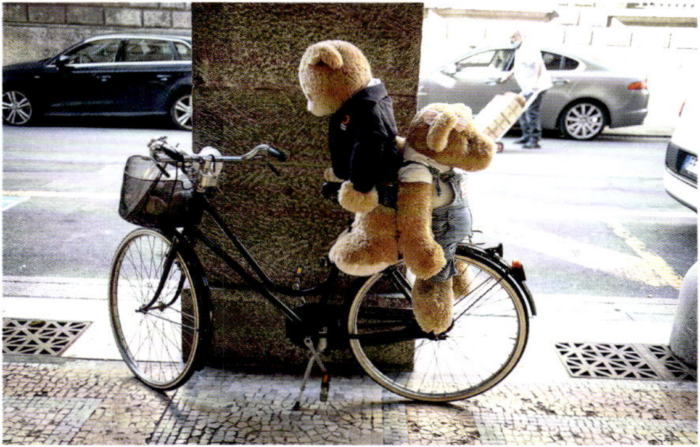

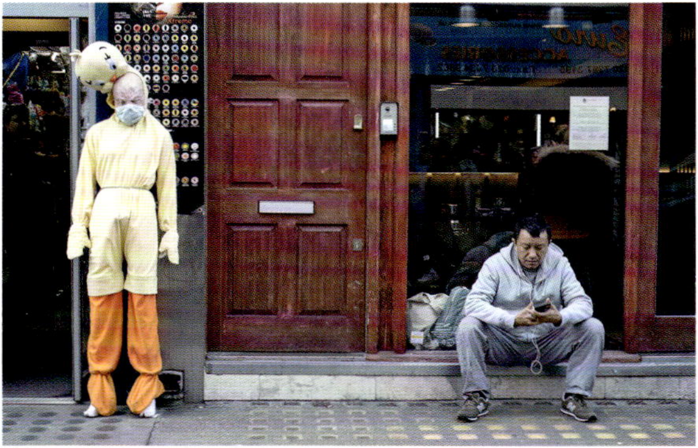

HUNTING VS. FISHING

Are you a hunter or a fisher? The hunter is constantly on the move, looking for subjects and tracking down opportunities. The fisher has a more considered approach, maybe finding a suitable background and then waiting for the right scene to develop in front of it. To be a good fisher, you need to be patient, constantly assessing the potential in your environment and visualizing the possibilities.

Both are valid approaches, and some people do both very well while others have a strong preference for either hunting or fishing; just be aware of the possibilities each approach can offer.

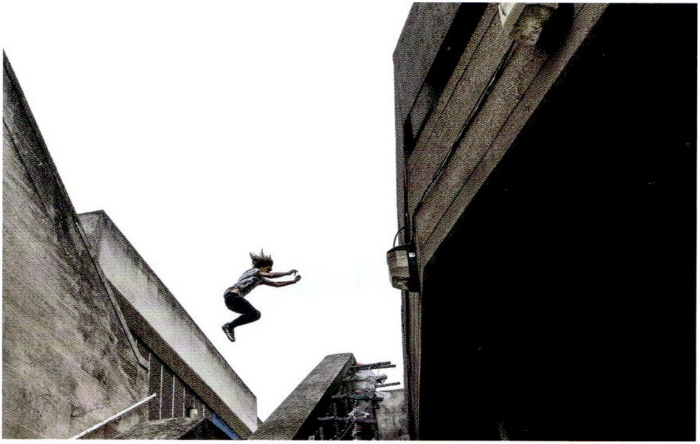

WHERE TO SHOOT?

Don't worry too much about finding the best or "iconic" locations—just head for where there is activity, light, and people. Bear these points in mind when deciding where to shoot.

Shoot in Busy Locations

You need places where there's plenty happening rather than quiet back streets; more activity equals more shooting opportunities.

Find Good Light

Contrasty light gives you more options. Don't be afraid of shooting in harsh sunlight.

Work the Scene

Once you've found a good location, stay there! Don't give up on it too soon; exploit all the angles, and walk around in search of the best backgrounds and good light. Be patient!

Get to Know the Rhythm and Feel of an Area

There's a lot to be said for getting to know areas really well—this will help you "feel" when a good shot is about to happen.

Go at Different Times of the Day

Remember that locations will have a different look and vibe at different times of day, so make a note of locations with potential and revisit them when conditions may be more favorable.

Watch the Background

Unless the background adds useful context to the composition, look for clean and uncluttered backgrounds to allow your subject to stand out.

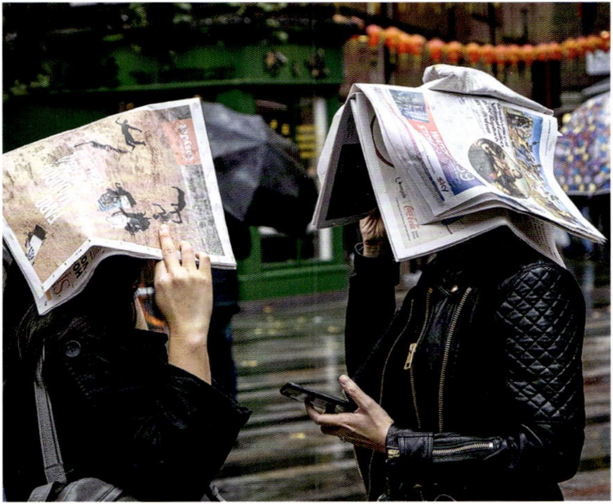

Opportunities Abound

You can do this anywhere, and you certainly don't need a big city for your street photography. Anywhere with people will work—even a small town or village. You just have to manage your expectations and be prepared to shoot a different style of street photography—maybe with more of a documentary focus.

BLACK & WHITE OR COLOR?

This is the big question. Street photography is usually all about authenticity; we live in a colorful world and color is certainly more "authentic" for street phctography. Black & white, however, has a significant following.

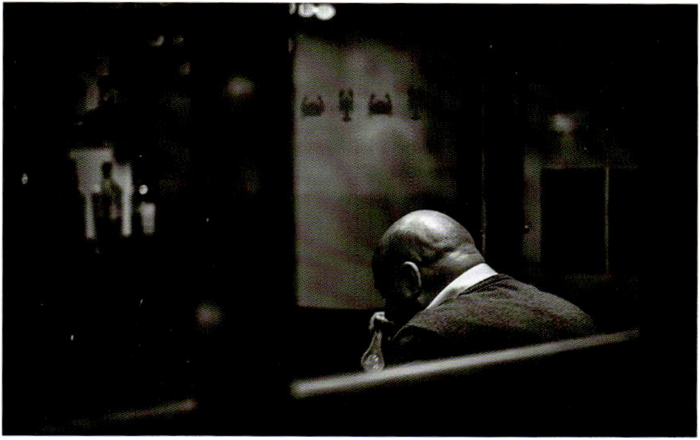

The decision to shoot in black & white should be made before you press the shutter—not as an afterthought. I don't think it's good practice to try to resuscitate a bad color shot by converting it to black & white—it'll usually end up looking like a bad black & white shot. So back to the question: When would I use black & white? I'd probably use it for a project, and as a deliberate aesthetic choice.

SHOOT THE STREETS AT NIGHT

Once you get the hang of some basics, try hitting the streets at night. It is actually quite easy and great fun. Think neon lights, shop windows, reflections, car lights, bars, restaurants, people having fun...there is masses of material to explore.

There's no reason that shooting in the dark should be any more difficult than daylight shooting, but there are some different technical and practical considerations to take into account. Here are seven tips for shooting street photography at night.

Find Good Light

Firstly, find a good light source, then build a composition around that. Aim for good contrast, with well-defined areas of light and dark—like the chiaroscuro effect in painting. You should think like a moth, seeking out lights all the time.

Understand the Effects of the Light

Ask yourself what you want the picture to say. What sort of mood or feel are you aiming to create? Now look at that light source: Does it suit the mood? Are the shadows sharp or less well defined? Is the light high or low intensity? What's the temperature of the light like: Is it warm or cool? Also consider the spread of the light. How does it cover your subject?

Use the Right Settings

Try these settings for shooting at night:

- ISO 3200
- Aperture Priority mode
- Wide open aperture (such as f/2)

Don't worry about using a high ISO—you need to get lots of light into the camera. Always shoot in RAW with the white balance on Auto.

Create Mystery

The nighttime is dark, foreboding, sometimes scary—and it's often mysterious. So you have the perfect opportunity to bring some of that mystery to your images, leaving the viewer thinking, "What if...?" This concept of holding something back, not revealing everything in a scene, is one of the things that will help you create a sense of mystery.

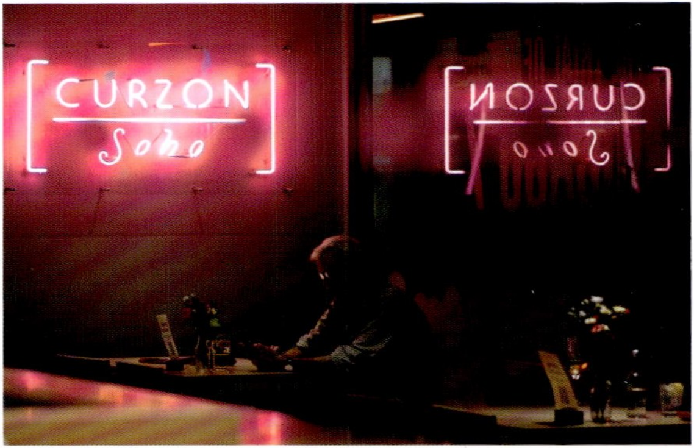

Aim for Dark Images

Cameras have a tendency to want to brighten things up, and the danger is that a night shot can end up looking like a daytime shot—and this is where your Exposure Compensation dial comes in handy. Try underexposing by 1 or 2 stops for a realistic nightscape.

Create Layered Images

Layers will add depth to your images. For example, try to use café windows that are reflecting the lights outside or perhaps have moisture on them. By also finding places where there is something interesting happening behind the glass, you can use this to create striking multi-layered photos which have real depth.

Stay Safe

Take more care at night than you would during the day. You'll be a little more exposed so be aware of who is around you and always have an "escape route" in mind. Try to stick to busier areas, and don't go down dark, quiet alleys alone. Shooting with a buddy or in a small group is often the best option at night.

04 STREET PORTRAITS

A street portrait is a posed, rather than candid, portrait of a stranger on the street. Typically, you'll see someone who looks interesting and ask them if you can take their portrait. And, if you're new to this, you'll probably be surprised by their reaction: 9 out of 10 readily say "yes." So far, so good, but is this truly "street photography"? It's a matter for debate, and it's probably in the margins of what we think of as being street photography—but it's a useful skill to have in your toolbox and great fun to do.

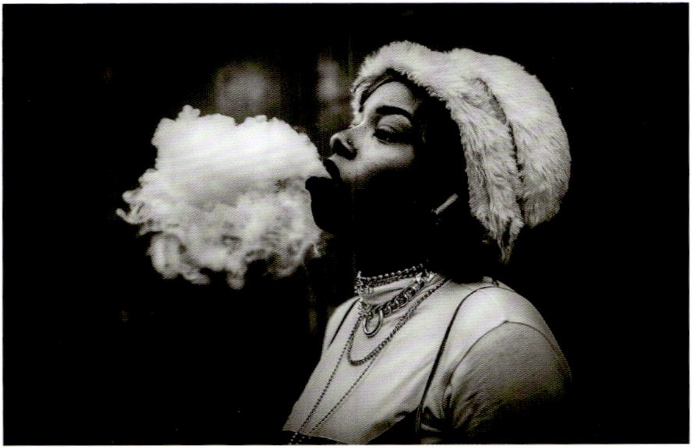

Have a Plan

Set yourself some objectives. Maybe you could treat this as a project, photographing a particular type of person—or at a specific location. Sometimes it's helpful to decide on a common style for the portraits. For example, do you want people to pose to your direction, or will you just snap away while you're chatting to them? Will the background be in or out of focus? Will it be an environmental portrait where the background plays a crucial role? Will the shots be close-up, half-length, or full-length? Will your subjects be looking to camera or off camera?

Choose the Right Subject

A great way to get started is to go for people who look good—who have made an effort. It could be fabulous clothes, great hair, an unusual hat, lots of tattoos—whatever it is, they're likely to be proud of it. And that usually means they want to show it off and will happily pose for you.

Just Go for It!

When you've found that ideal subject, don't hesitate—that initial moment of uncertainly can sap your confidence and could make you look shifty. When you see a likely subject, just go for it. A simple "Can I take your picture?" usually does the trick.

Get Your Approach Right

Make sure you approach people in a really relaxed manner and with a smile on your face. If you seem relaxed, they'll relax; if you seem nervous and shifty, they'll be starting to have doubts. Smiling is infectious, and this initial warmth will go a long way to helping get a successful portrait. So just relax!

Take Rejection on the Chin

Rejection is all part of the game—part of the fun, even. Put it aside and move on.

Think about the Light

Scout around for great light. Remember, you're in control of the situation so you need to be super-aware of where the good light is happening and be prepared to move your subject toward it. Some people use flash or carry a small collapsible white reflector in their bag—this can be great for directing some natural light into the face.

Take Control

When they're posing for a picture, most folks are far more comfortable being directed—"look over there" or "drop your right arm down a bit" or "stand just next to that pillar." If your subjects are being told what to do, they'll feel less awkward and less self-conscious.

Don't Rush It!

Trying to get it all over with as quickly as possible will add to the nervousness—of you and possibly of your subject—and you'll always be disappointed that you didn't get the best possible outcome from the situation. Take your time and get the shot.

Be Generous

I'll often offer to send the subject a copy of the image, which is a nice quid pro quo for their time and attention. You could also consider having an instant camera with you (I use a Fujifilm Instax); it takes just a few seconds to take that extra shot, and most people love getting that little print in their hands.

Have Some Business Cards Made

This will not only make you feel more "authentic" but it's also a demonstration of your legitimacy as a photographer. I've known the humble little card to make the difference between acceptance and rejection.

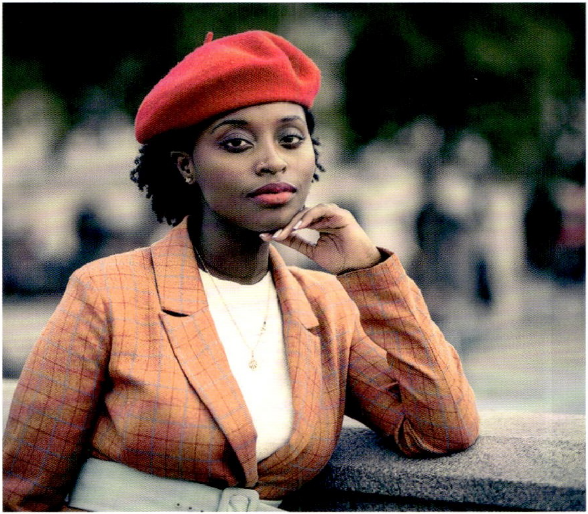

WHAT GEAR TO USE FOR STREET PORTRAITS?

It doesn't really matter what sort of camera you use, but do try to be consistent. If you're aiming to produce a body of work, use the same lens throughout the project. Use a longer lens for street portraits—50mm or 85mm is ideal—and shoot with a wide maximum aperture, such as f/2, f/1.4, or f/1.2. Some people use flash but I much prefer to make the most of soft available light.

Whatever gear you use, the most important thing is that you're completely familiar with it and confident using it. Once you start fumbling with settings or dithering about what to do, your subject will start to doubt your competence and will lose interest.

Enjoy the experience!

Once you get over the initial reticence or nerves, taking street portraits should be a spontaneous, joyful experience. It leads to some great encounters and interesting conversations—and you nearly always finish the shoot with a big smile on your face.

05 SHOOT PROJECTS

WHAT IS A PROJECT?

A project is a collection of images—a distinct body of work—generated around a specific theme with a kind of visual "glue" that bonds the images together. If storytelling is your thing, projects allow you to build a strong narrative, using a cohesive set of images to tell a story.

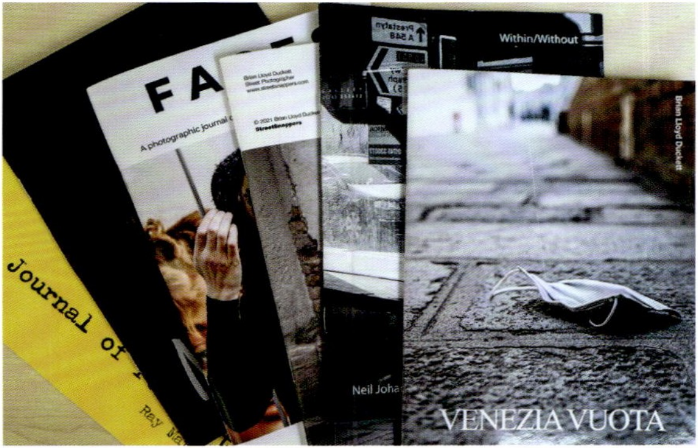

Projects can be very simple, such as "Dogs in New York," or they can be more in-depth and possibly lean towards documentary photography. If this is a new way of working for you, keep it simple to start with and embark on a project you're confident you can complete.

If you're serious about your street photography, projects will take you in a new and exciting direction.

WHY SHOOT PROJECTS?

When we struggle to find sufficiently interesting subject matter, we often resort to randomness: pictures of random people, in random places, doing random things. This all too easily becomes boring street photography! There is no sense of narrative, no theme, and no connection between the images. So, to add real impact to your work, organize your shooting around projects.

Projects Give You Focus and Direction

On days when you can find little inspiration or motivation, or when there is nothing happening, working on a project gives you the impetus to go out and shoot in an organized manner.

Projects Can Provide You with a Clear End Game

However you choose to bring the project to life, it will spur you on to produce a tangible, worthy body of work.

Projects Allow You to Tell a Story

While it is perfectly possible to tell a story using a single image, think about how much more powerful that story can be if told using a cohesive set of images, edited and sequenced in a logical order and taking the viewer on a structured journey.

Projects Provide a Sense of Achievement

One of the most satisfying outcomes of a project is to share your work, and there's a real sense of achievement in seeing your images in a gallery, on a website, or in the pages of a book.

FINDING INSPIRATION

Where do you get the ideas for a project from? Where do you find the creative inspiration? Quite often, an idea will come from pictures you've already taken. Or maybe you'll take inspiration from someone else's work—of course, fully copying another photographer's ideas isn't the way to do it, but taking one little flicker of inspiration is all you need. Alternatively, you could base your project on something you're interested in outside of photography. It could be related to music, or sport, or a particular place.

Does it matter if it's been done before? No, as long as you do it *differently* and with your own creative interpretation.

BRINGING YOUR PROJECT TO LIFE

The first point to make here is that you don't necessarily *need* an outlet for your project. It can be purely for your own enjoyment and creative fulfilment—an exercise in self-satisfaction and self-indulgence. Assuming you want other people to see your work, however, you have a basic choice to make: you can print your project or you can show it digitally.

Print Options

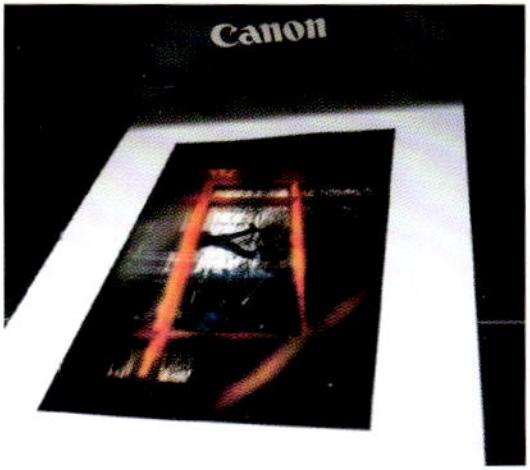

In its simplest form, your project could come to life as a set of prints. You could display the pictures as an exhibition on the walls of your local coffee shop—or even in a gallery—or just on your dining room wall.

Photobooks are now popular and are a cost-effective way to publicize your projects. There are numerous publishing companies that will produce anything from one or two copies to thousands, and the results can look stunning.

A great alternative to producing a book is the smaller zine. These are quick, easy, and cheap to produce and are another great way to get your project out there; you can even sell your zines online, through galleries, or at photo fairs.

Digital Options

In its simplest form, your project could be shown as a section on your website or as a blog post. Then there's social media—with all the benefits of sharing—and this social amplification can really give oxygen to your project, bringing it to a much bigger audience and opening up all sorts of other possibilities.

WHAT NEXT?

Of course, projects are not the only way forward with your street photography. Sometimes it's good to just relax, empty your mind, and rely on those unexpected little opportunities that you stumble across—randomness isn't always a bad thing! However, if you adopt the project approach, you will almost certainly find some extra drive and motivation that will help take your street photography to a new level.

So start with one simple project—nothing too ambitious—and aim to have two or three on the go within a year. It's a game-changer!

The images shown on the following page were part of a short project called *"Venezia Vuota"* (Empty Venice), which highlighted the quietness and serenity of this usually frenetic city in the post-pandemic months. The project was made into a zine and set of fine art prints.

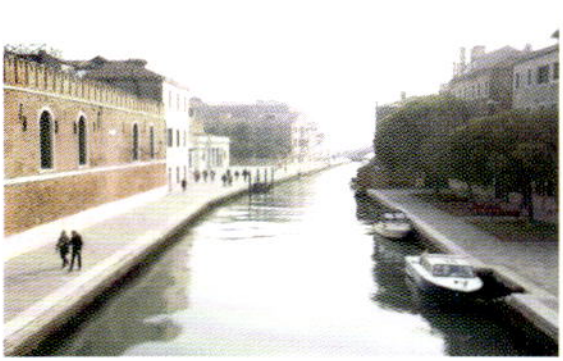
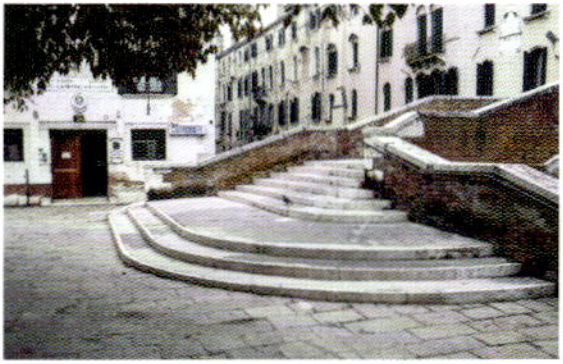
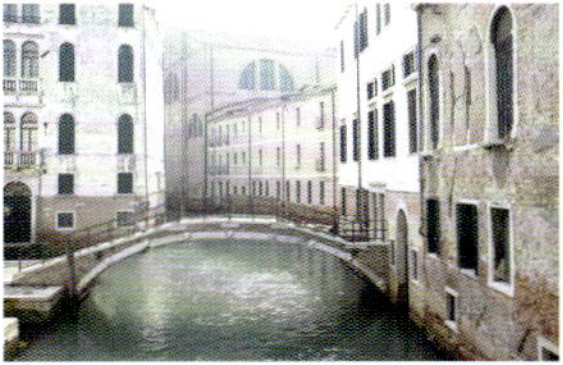
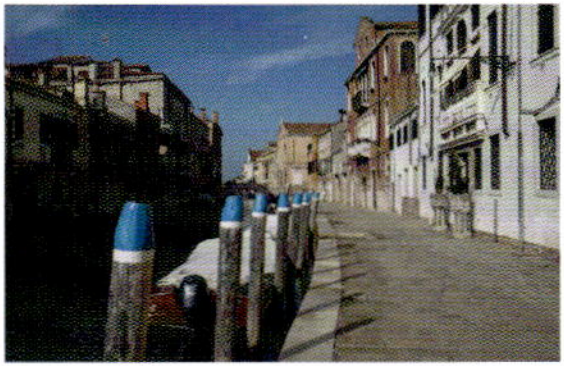
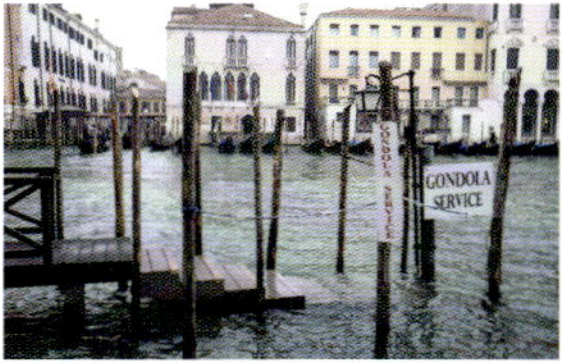
GONDOLA
SERVICE
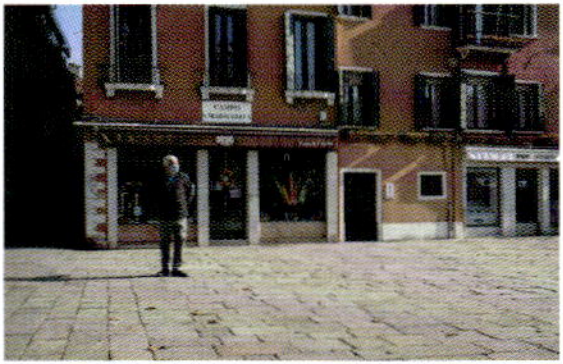

06 BUILD YOUR CONFIDENCE

12 TIPS TO BANISH THE FEAR FACTOR

Some of us find street photography easy, others find it uncomfortable or even scary. We often have fears about being confronted or challenged, or we have concerns about what people will think of us. The good news is that, even if the thought of shooting strangers terrifies you, there are plenty of things you can do to increase your comfort and confidence as a street photographer.

Remember—You're Doing Nothing Wrong

Have it fixed in your mind that taking pictures is a perfectly normal activity and you're not doing anything wrong. If your motives and intentions are clear then you should shoot with confidence.

Be Friendly

Appear to be open, friendly, and relaxed—not furtive or looking like you're up to no good. If you have the right demeanor, you'll have a much easier time on the streets.

Have a "Back Story" or a Script

Be prepared to explain yourself and to chat about what you're doing. This should help reassure people (and you!) that you're a legitimate photographer.

Blend In and Don't Look Like a Photographer

Travel light with a small bag and a small camera, and you'll look more like a harmless tourist.

Stay Back

While it's generally good practice to get up close, start off by shooting a little further away, perhaps with an 85mm lens, then moving down to a 50mm, then to a 35mm or wider. Your confidence should increase with time and practice.

Shoot "Past" People

Pretend you're shooting something in the background, way beyond the people in front of you.

Shoot Quickly

Have your camera set up and ready, and don't mess around with zooming, composition, or settings. Take your picture quickly and move away.

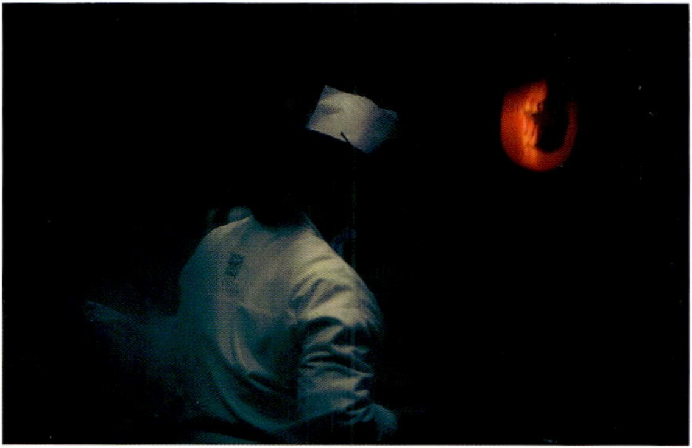

Shoot from the Hip

This is not something to be done all the time but can help if you want to go unnoticed. Shooting from waist level is easier if you have a flip screen, but with practice it will work with any camera.

Use a Wide Lens

A lens of 28mm or wider will take in so much of the scene that it's easy to get very close to people without them realizing it's them you're interested in.

Shoot in "Panning" Mode

Pretend you're shooting a video, panning across a scene, and press the shutter button at the crucial moment.

Know the Law

Knowledge breeds confidence, and you'll feel much better if you're certain that what you're doing is 100% legal.

Avoid Eye Contact

This is the killer tip and a game-changer. If you avoid eye contact, you're far less likely to have any confrontations or other engagements with the people you shoot. So don't make eye contact before, during, or after the shot.

DEALING WITH CONFRONTATION

"Confrontation" is perhaps a strong word: think of it more as "engagement." There will be times when someone stops you and asks, "Did you take my picture?"—and you need to know how to respond.

Bear in mind that people are usually asking out of curiosity rather than anger, so keep things relaxed and friendly; a warm smile can be quite disarming and will bring the temperature down a bit if the person seems unsettled.

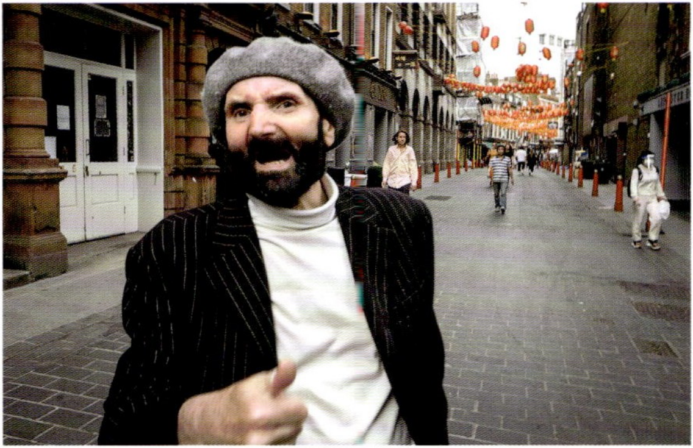

When confronted, you need two levels of response. The first, which works in most situations is a smile, say "thank you," and then move on; that's usually the end of the matter.

But sometimes the person will persevere and press you for a fuller response—and this is where the second response, your "script," comes in. Have a prepared response—something which you feel comfortable with and, of course, which is true. You could, for example, explain that you're a student of street photography and you're doing a project about that particular area or street.

Or you could say that you're just out practicing with your new camera. Whatever your story, learn it and be confident in delivering it.

SHOULD YOU DELETE AN IMAGE IF CONFRONTED?

Someone might occasionally ask you to delete an image, and your response should normally be "no." However, you should deal with each situation on its merits: if you feel uncomfortable, or in danger, or if you feel you may have really upset someone, then it's best to comply and delete the image. If your camera has two card slots, always shoot a backup to the second card so you'll have a copy in case you need to delete the original.

07 LAW & ETHICS

KNOW THE LAW!

A good knowledge of what you are allowed and not allowed to do as a street photographer is essential. The precise rules will differ according to where you are, and it's a good idea to check out the local laws for wherever you're shooting.

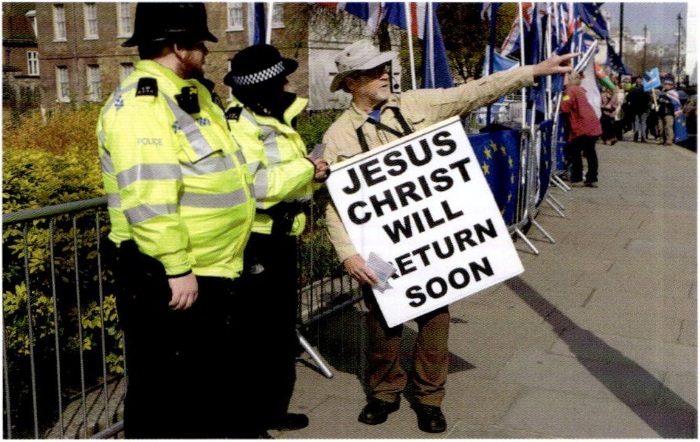

However, the basic principles are broadly similar in most countries, and provided you are shooting in a public place (such as the street, beach, park, etc.), you can take pictures of people, buildings, or objects without permission. The legal premise is usually that if a person is in a public place, they have no expectation of privacy and can therefore be photographed—whoever they are or whatever they're doing.

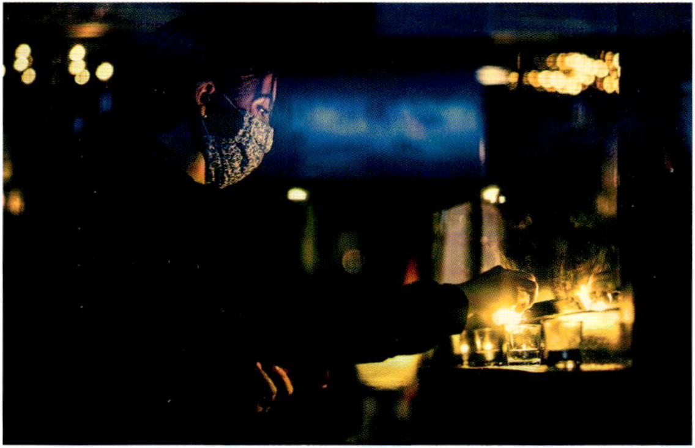

PUBLIC VS. PRIVATE

While the position regarding shooting in a public place is fairly clear, shooting in private is more complicated. Private places could include, for example, railway stations, galleries, cafés, or shopping malls, and the owners of these places have their own terms and conditions—one of which is often the prohibition of photography. It's not illegal to take pictures in such places, though you can expect to be asked to desist or perhaps leave the premises.

Most people would expect to have a higher expectation of privacy when in a private place, though it's a question of degree. If you're sitting in a café, this is a place the public has access to, and it could be said to be *reasonably* public, in which case you wouldn't normally have a problem taking pictures. However, if you were to photograph someone inside their house you could rightly expect a robust response.

USAGE

When it comes to getting your images out there, the legal situation varies enormously from country to country and, again, this is something you must check out before you publish. In many territories, unless your image is used for third party commercial use (which usually means advertising), you are free to publish—whether that means making prints, having an exhibition, producing books, or posting on social media. But do check first!

CHILDREN

It is usually legal to take pictures of children without their parents' consent, but do take care. We live in a paranoid world and your motives can easily be misconstrued. Wherever possible, speak to the parents (who are probably nearby) and get their consent *before* pressing the shutter.

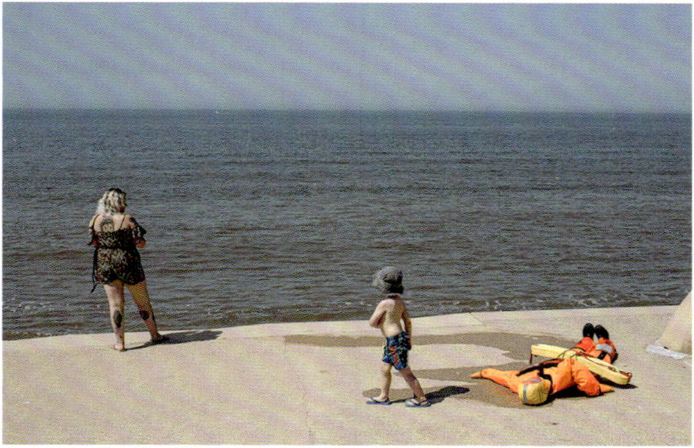

YOUR ETHICS

We all view the world in different ways, and we all have different ethical positions when it comes to street photography. However, most agree that we shouldn't take pictures of homeless, vulnerable, or distressed people. It's good practice to put yourself in the shoes of the person being photographed: how would you feel if the roles were reversed?